PORTRAIT OF
MONMOUTHSHIRE

Nick Jenkins

HALSGROVE

First published in Great Britain in 2009

British Library Cataloguing-in-Publication Data
A CIP record for this title is available from the British Library

ISBN 978 1 84114 889 2

HALSGROVE
Halsgrove House,
Ryelands Industrial Estate,
Bagley Road, Wellington, Somerset TA21 9PZ
Tel: 01823 653777   Fax: 01823 216796
email: sales@halsgrove.com

Part of the Halsgrove group of companies
Information on all Halsgrove titles is available at: www.halsgrove.com

Printed and bound in India on behalf of JFDI Print Services Ltd

Acknowledgements

For a change, I would like to dedicate *Portrait of Monmouthshire* to my good friends and colleagues at Gwynfa Camera Club, near Llantrisant, in south Wales. It is no exaggeration to say that, without their encouragement and support, this work simply would not have happened.

I am also once more grateful to the team at Halsgrove for giving me the opportunity to again show off the beauty of my home country of Wales (even if Monmouthshire was once a part of England!).

Photographer's Notes

I am never too sure just how helpful it is to pore over the technology used to take my pictures, preferring instead to lay the main emphasis on the combination of a good pair of legs and a seeing eye. Nevertheless, the following is a short summary of how I approach my photography, and with what!

Since *Portrait of Glamorgan* was published I have purchased a Nikon D300 digital camera, which has given me excellent results. All the pictures in the book were taken either on a Nikon F5 film camera, using Fuji Velvia 50ASA slide film, or on the Nikon digital camera, using mainly 4Gb Sandisk CF memory cards. Lenses (which are sometimes underutilised, at our peril) were all Nikon or Sigma, with focal lengths ranging from 17mm to 300mm. I invariably use a tripod; an excellent carbon fibre Gitzo generally, but on occasions where I want to get really close to a flower or similar I use a Uniloc tripod with a Benbo head. A spirit level keeps my horizons and skylines nice and straight (yes, I know it is possible to do this in Photoshop or other post processing products) as I try to place heavy emphasis on getting it right in the camera. I try to limit the use of filters, preferring to capture 'what is', but do make use of polarisers, and neutral density graduated filters to either even-up the exposure if the sky is too bright or simply to enhance a stormy cloudscape. And all this packs neatly into a Lowepro All Weather Nature Trekker camera rucksack for ease of carrying.

I very often walk around an area before even taking my first shot, seeking out the most interesting angle and the best direction of the light. I will also walk a complete 360 degree circle around the object or location I am photographing, where possible, before I photograph it, often to the amusement/amazement of passers by. And I will always look behind me after I have pressed the shutter as you just never know what you might be missing.

The light? Well, sometimes I like to think I plan around it, but if the truth be told, it usually just happens. Being there in the first place is, of course, the key. Photographers make their own luck.

In the end it is down to individual likes and dislikes. I do so hope you have enjoyed this portfolio of Monmouthshire – there were so many more photographs I could have selected, and no doubt there will be some favourites of yours missing, but all things must draw to an end eventually.

LOCATION MAPS – Monmouthshire

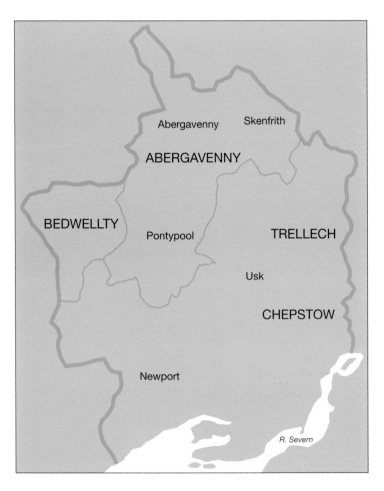

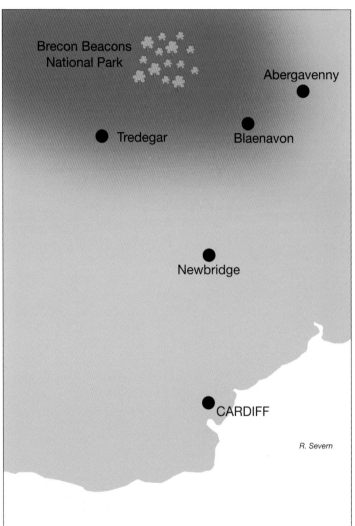

Introduction

The Monmouthshire of today sits in the very south-east corner of Wales, and borders Gloucestershire and Herefordshire. It is, and always has been, a border county, although on which side of the border has often caused confusion, oscillating between England and Wales!

The county of Monmouthshire itself was created in 1536 and was an amalgamation of the old Norman Marcher Lordships of Newport, Abergavenny, Monmouth, Chepstow, Caerleon and Usk. These Marcher Lordships were originally set up by William the Conqueror to contain the Welsh and prevent skirmishes into England. The Lords who were allocated these tracts of land were all but autonomous in the way they ruled their little kingdoms.

However, the doubts over whether Monmouthshire sat in England or Wales started in 1543 when it was omitted from the second Act of Union which established the Court of Great Session legal system in Wales. Consequently, a number of laws that were passed covering Wales were deemed not to be applicable in Monmouthshire, for example the closure of Public Houses on Sundays. The queue of Sunday drinkers across the border can be imagined! I can clearly recall being taken on family trips into England to visit Chepstow Castle and Tintern Abbey (at a very young age, of course!).

In 1974, along with many other counties in Wales, the county of Monmouthshire was done away with and replaced by the county of Gwent. This placed it firmly and unequivocally in Wales. Gwent covered a large area stretching from what we now know as the Heads of the Valleys road (the A465) in the north across and up to the border village of Llangua (again on the A465 Hereford road) and back to Chepstow and along to just short of Cardiff. The sheer range and variety of countryside and landscapes was enormous, ranging from the western industrial valleys of the Rivers Sirhowy, Tyleri, Lwyd and Ebbw to the town (now a city) of Newport, the flat marshes of the coast butting onto the River Severn and the upland Black Mountains as part of the Brecon Beacons National Park. Also included are the large agricultural areas around Monmouth, Usk and Abergavenny so that, all in all, Gwent was a county of some fair size and complexity.

The year 1996 brought with it more boundary changes and Gwent disappeared completely to be replaced, along with a number of other Unitary Authorities, by . . . wait for it . . . Monmouthshire. This Monmouthshire, however, was a much reduced version and comprises mainly the rural and agricultural south and east areas of old Gwent, and firmly excluding the valleys and Newport.

Our *Portrait of Monmouthshire* will go back a little in time to explore the many fascinating aspects of this corner of Wales. We will visit the historical heritage treasures of the industrial areas in Blaenavon, including both the World Heritage ironworks and Big Pit. We will also explore the Black Mountains with the hidden church of Partrishow and Llanthony Priory in the border valley of Ewyas. We will discover castles such as Chepstow (the first substantial stone castle to be built in Britain), Raglan and the three border castles of Skenfrith, Grosmont and White Castle and we will explore the stunning beauty of the Wye Valley, forming, along parts of its length, the boundary between England and Wales.

This, once more, has been a real journey of revelation for me. Certainly I had drawn up a list of 'must visit' locations and each time I duly visited I found myself being drawn in different directions to explore and discover. On numerous occasions I set out with a destination firmly in my mind, never to reach it as a result of being (very happily) sidetracked! If I spot a road sign leading to a village I have never heard of you can bet your bottom dollar that I will be distracted in that direction and have to revisit my original plan another day.

Anyway, I have had a wonderful time putting together this portfolio of 'old' Monmouthshire and sincerely hope that you will also enjoy the journey. As is always the case, I will have omitted places that the reader will clamour to see and for that I apologise in anticipation. I have, however, made every effort to show the sheer variety of views and locations in this county contained within Wales . . . for the moment.

**Llandewi Fach,
Black Letter Box**
I spotted this built into the wall of the Old Rectory, and cannot recall ever having seen one this colour before.

Abergavenny Market Hall
This well known Abergavenny icon, with its copper-roofed
clock tower built in the 1870s, is used regularly to
hold markets for both food and crafts.

Llanfoist Wharf
Once a very busy spot during the Industrial Revolution, it is now a
peaceful site for mooring narrowboats and enjoying a quiet walk.

Babel Chapel, Cwmfelinfach

Located in the Sirhowy Valley, this tiny chapel is the resting place of the nineteenth-century
Welsh poet William Thomas (1832–1878), better known by his welsh pseudonym of Islwyn.

Babel Chapel, Headstones
I was amazed at just how closely the headstones in this tiny graveyard had been packed in.

Church, Kemeys Commander
Yet another discovery for me.
I had never heard of
Kemeys Commander before.

Betws Newydd Church
This ancient little church, buried away in the Monmouthshire countryside, is a real discovery.
It is dedicated to Saint Aidan, or Aedan of Llawhaden, in Pembrokeshire.

**Betws Newydd
Church, Interior**
The interior of the church initially seems quite dark until the eyes settle. When they do they land right on the wonderful fifteenth-century carved rood screen.

Blackwood – Chartist Bridge
Opened in 2005, the bridge stands as a reminder of the close links that Blackwood
and Oakdale had with the Chartist Movement and uprisings in the late 1830s.

Garn Cottages, Blaenavon
Photographed from the line of the Pontypool and Blaenavon Railway I felt that the viewpoint
showed the bleakness of this upland, and once heavily industrialised area.

Garn Ponds, Blaenavon
The ponds have now been restored and put back to nature. When I was here a heron flew just over my head.

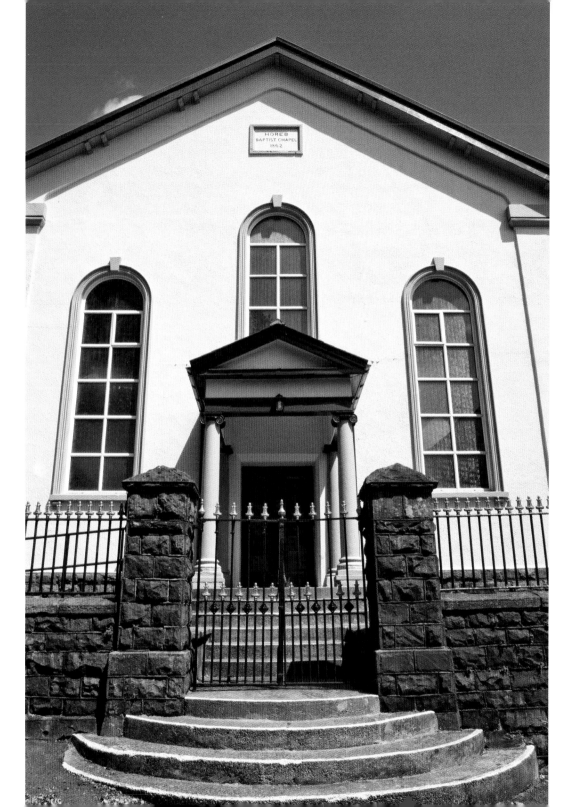

Blaenavon, Horeb Baptist Chapel
Part of the World Heritage Site, Horeb was opened in 1863 and is said to have been built in the shape of an industrial engine house.

Ironworks Cottages, Blaenavon

Recently seen as the location for a 'reality TV' documentary, these cottages have been well restored
to give a real flavour of what it was like to live here when the ironworks were in full production.

Blaenavon Post Office
In a period when Post Offices seem to be under siege it was wonderful
to see how busy this one was – and their pasties are first class!

Blaenavon Workingmen's Hall
Many of the Welsh valleys had a Workingmen's Hall as a vital part of the community.
The hall in Blaenavon is a superb example of industrial Wales architecture and was paid for by the miners.

Keepers Pond
The pond was built around 1894 to supply water
to the nearby Garn Ddyrys forges. The name is said to
have been derived from the fact that, nearby, the
Earl of Abergavenny's gamekeeper had his cottage.

Foxhunter's Grave, Blorenge
This is where Foxhunter, the Olympic champion horse, ridden by Colonel Harry Llewellyn was buried
in 1959 – a spot so loved by the Colonel that his ashes were scattered near here too.

River Wye near Bigsweir Bridge

Bigsweir Bridge near Llandogo
Photographed on a very cold but atmospheric morning when all was calm and still and the River Wye appeared motionless.

Brockweir Bridge
This road bridge forms the border crossing between England and Wales.
The shot was taken from the path of the Wye Valley Walk.

Near Brockweir in Autumn
The autumn colours were really vibrant when I walked this section of the Wye Valley Walk at Brockweir.

Caerwent Roman Town Walls

Caerwent was built by the Romans as a settlement for the Silures, a tribe who gave them quite a bit of gip when they invaded. The walls are a clear reminder of the Roman presence in Monmouthshire.

Capel y Ffin Church
This quaint little whitewashed church was referred to by the
Victorian diarist Francis Kilvert as looking like a stout grey owl.

Capel y Ffin Chapel
Might this be the true chapel of Capel y Ffin? Hidden back from the church,
the Methodist Chapel is seldom visited by passing visitors.

Chepstow, Iron Bridge
This wonderful cast iron bridge, forming the border between England
and Wales, was opened in 1816 amidst much pomp and ceremony.

Chepstow Castle
The oldest surviving stone fortification in Britain,
Chepstow Castle was the springboard for the Normans into Wales.
Building started in 1067, not long after the Norman Conquest!

Forge Row Cottages, Cwmavon
I almost drove straight past this wonderful row of old miners' cottages as I made my way
to Blaenavon. To me they epitomise the way folk would have lived, with the large
vegetable plots in the front and the cobbled alley leading past the front doors.

St George Church, Cwmyoy
Surely best known for being built on a landslip area, this solid little church leans at all angles in all directions.

Farmland near Skenfrith
Home to one of the three castles in the 'triangle' Skenfrith is surrounded by
agricultural landscapes and wooded hills. This scene is typical.

Fisherman at Goldcliffe
The Monmouthshire coast is nowhere truly beautiful but there is a certain charm here… and fishermen seem to like it.

Horse Rings, Folly Tower

Left:
Pontypool, Folly Tower
A folly built by the Hanbury family around the mid 1700s,
the Tower was demolished in 1940 as it was feared to be a landmark
for German bombers seeking the ordnance factory at nearby Glascoed.

Llandegfedd Reservoir, Pontypool
Run as a country park, the reservoir has facilities for a range of watersports including canoeing and fishing.

Goldcliff Shoreline
The coastline to the east of Newport is very flat and prone to
flooding, hence the floodwall here. Many years ago it was popular
to catch salmon in traps along this stretch of shoreline – indeed
some folk still continue this ancient form of fishing.

Right:
Willows near Goldcliff
I love the way that the willows just seem to shoot upwards out of the reeds.

Black Mountains View
This shot was taken from above the Grwyne Fechan Valley on a beautiful
autumn morning – the dappled landscape just cried out to be recorded!

Grwyne Fechan Valley
This narrow wooded valley lies deep in the Black Mountains. Across
the valley lie the heights of Waun Fach and Pen y Gadair Fawr.

Tredegar Iron Clock
Raised in 1858 this proud clock stands as
a reminder of Tredegar's existence and growth.

Right:
Bedwellty House, Tredegar – Band Stand
Built in 1818 for the South Wales ironmaster, Samuel Homfray,
Bedwellty House and grounds are now maintained by
Blaenau Gwent Borough Council. The grounds are open to the public.

Tredegar – Cefn Golau Cholera Cemetery
The bleak location of the cemetery, on a hillside away from the centre of
population, reminds us just how grim life was in the valleys of the nineteenth century.

Grosmont Castle
Along with Skenfrith and White Castle, Grosmont was built
by the Normans to protect one of the key routes into and out
of South Wales. It is believed to date from around 1070.

Skenfrith Castle
Along with White Castle and Grosmont (which all connect to make
a very good walk) Skenfrith Castle was one of the triangle of
three guarding the English/Welsh border in Norman times.

Skenfrith Church
This wonderful rural church just sits so well next to Skenfrith Castle.

White Castle, Llantilio Crosseny
Once believed to have been painted or plastered white, this squat and
solid castle formed part of the 'three castles' line of defence into Wales.

Clydach Gorge
At the time of writing
a debate rages as to the
future of this deep and
heavily wooded
beech gorge, as the
'rebuild' of the Heads
of the Valleys road
progresses apace.

Railway Street, Llanhilleth

I didn't really know Llanhilleth but following some web enquiries I had so many replies from present and past inhabitants I soon realised what a thriving community exists. There is a superb (and recently restored) Miners' Institute here.

Train leaving Llanhilleth
Llanhilleth, in the Ebbw Valley, seems to have a real buzz and sense of community
about it, and the recently reopened railway has made access much more easy.

St Illtyd's Church, Llanhilleth
Sitting atop the hillside above Llanhilleth this seldom used and isolated church has
a wonderful 'back to nature' graveyard, full of poppies and daisies in the summer.

Llanelly Church
The churchyard is tended in such a way that wildlife can thrive here, both flora and fauna. The wildness of the place somehow suits it far better than a neat manicure.

Llanfihangel Crucorney Church
When I visited this old church
the west end was not roofed. This
has since been restored. The
cherry blossom just lifted the
scene and added a splash
of colour.

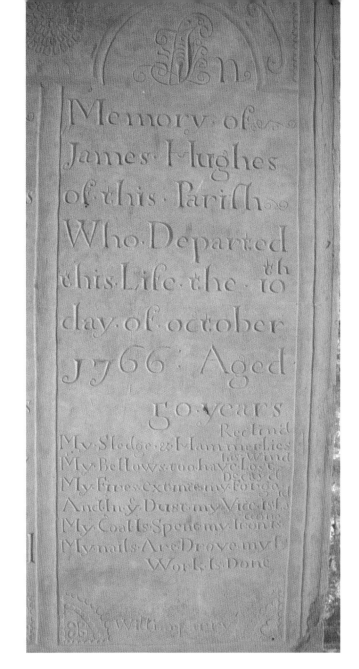

Epitaph, Llanfihangel Church

This wonderful epitaph lies on a headstone just inside the church porch and is well worth reading.

Skirrid Inn
This superb old inn in Llanfihangel Crucorney is claimed to be the oldest in Wales.
When visiting ask to see the 'hanging stairs' and rope, where summary justice was once dispensed!

Trostrey Church

This remote church sits some distance away from Trostrey, near Betws Newydd, but offers superb views across rolling countryside. Also visible nearby is the newly rebuilt windmill.

Lane near Trostrey

Trostrey is a small farming community near Betws Newydd. To me, this
lane typifies the quiet rural setting in this part of Monmouthshire.

Left:
Farmland, Trostrey

Rainbow near Little Skirrid
On a visit to nearby Llanfihangell Crucorney one afternoon, I spotted this odd partial rainbow over the little barn.

Llanthony Priory

This jewel of a priory, set in the Vale of Ewyas, is one of the oldest houses of Augustinian Canons in Britain.
It was built in the twelfth century by William de Lacy and its peaceful setting belies its turbulent history.

St David's Church, Llanthony
Dedicated to the patron saint of Wales, it is believed
he once had a small monastic cell on this spot.

Right:
Llanthony Valley
Also known, more properly, as the Vale of Ewyas, this remote and
deep valley is almost on the border with Herefordshire and England.

Lower Machen Church
Part of a pretty little village, bypassed by the route from Newport to Caerphilly.

The River Wye at Monmouth
This stretch of the Wye is very popular with rowers and plays host to the local celebration of the Monmouth raft race.

Monmouth Agincourt Square

Charles Rolls, Monmouth
Situated just in front of
the Town Hall this statue
is the town's recognition
of this world famous car
manufacturer and aviator
and his Monmouth roots.
The statue is by
Goscombe John.

Monmouth Castle
Or rather, what little is now left of it.

St Thomas Cross, Monmouth
This ancient preaching cross is just to the west of the Monnow Bridge.

Dixton Church, Monmouth
This pretty little church outside Monmouth lies
almost on the banks of the River Wye.

Left:
The Kymin, Monmouth
This superb viewpoint plays host to a two-storey circular
banqueting house, dating from 1794, paid for by a group
of Monmouth's gentlemen, 'The Kymin Club'.

Monmouth Monnow Bridge
This wonderful thirteenth-century construction is Monmouth's
pride and joy, being the only remaining fortified
medieval bridge in Britain.

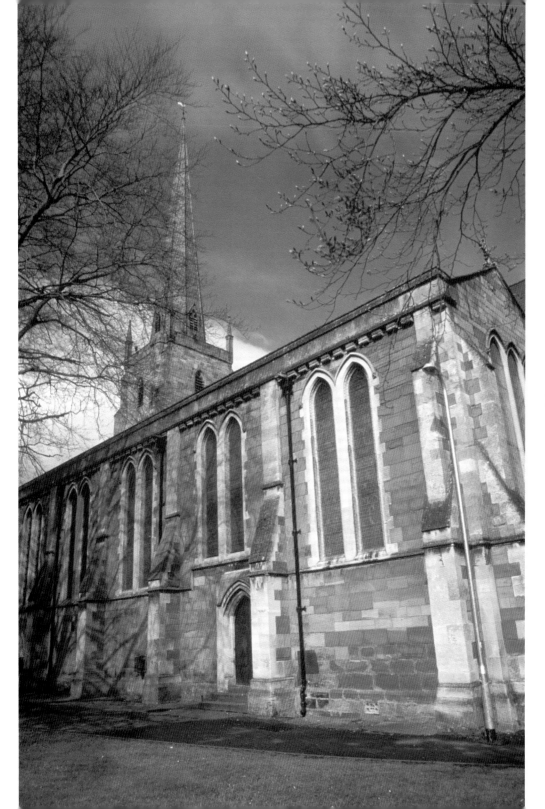

St Mary's Church, Monmouth
This priory church in the heart of
Monmouth was remodelled during
Victorian times from its original
Georgian roots.

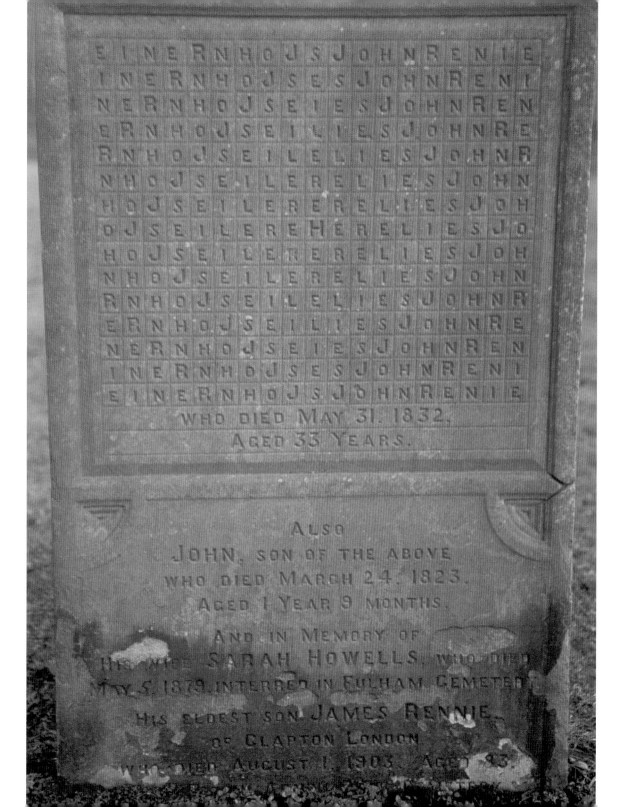

John Renie's Monument, Monmouth
Look carefully and you can see the puzzle!

River Monnow at Monmouth
Joining the River Wye at Monmouth, the Monnow (or, in Welsh, the Afon Mynwy – swift water) forms for part of its length the border between England and Wales.

Mynydd Alltir Fawr
More a hillside than a mountain the views from here are rewarding, showing the rural landscape to its full effect.

Newport Transporter Bridge
This incredible structure is one of only a handful of such bridges throughout the world still working.

Dragonfly on Fourteen Locks
This amazing sculpture, cast in bronze, was unveiled in 2001 and if you examine it carefully you can see a collage of parts of canal boats and other industrial 'bits', aiming to evoke memories of industrial South Wales.

Rainbow at Tredegar House
I was struck by the strength of this rainbow
when contrasted with the wrought iron gates
of the Tredegar House old entrance.

Oak Tree, Skenfrith
This solitary tree on the horizon was calling out to be photographed.

Pantygelli Chapel
This poor and neglected chapel near Abergavenny is almost totally
consumed by Nature; only the entrance door is fully visible.

Partrishow Church

Perhaps best known for its medieval rood screen, Partrishow Church is hidden away in the folds of the Black Mountains near Forest Coal Pit, just waiting to be discovered.

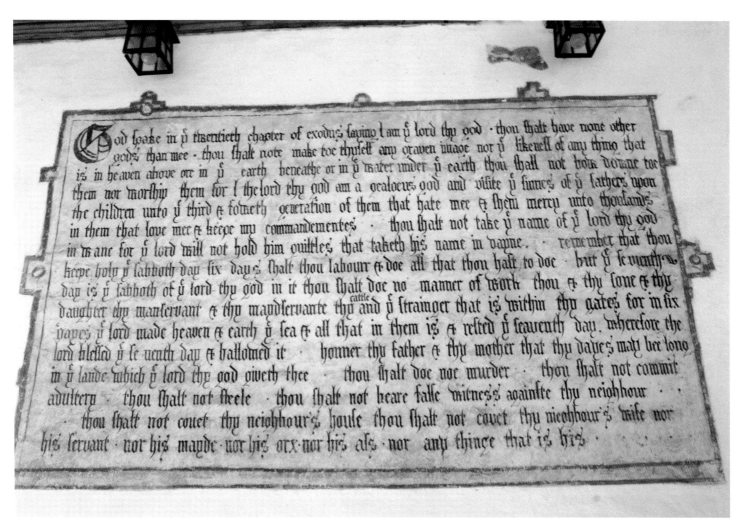

Notice how the word 'cattle' was originally omitted.

Pasture near
Partrishow Church

Rainbow near Cwmbran
Another of my short, sharp, stops; rainbows seldom last long.

St Thomas the Apostle Church, Redwick
The largest church on the Caldicot Levels, St Thomas' Church is full of interest
for the visitor, including an uncommon 'full immersion' baptism pool.

Right:
River Wye at Tintern
With its source under Pumlumon in Mid Wales, the Wye is the fifth longest river in the UK.

Boat Moored on the Wye at Tintern
This boat struck me as unusual in that it appeared to be quite old in its design.

Sirhowy Valley Cycle Route
Part of the National Cycle
Route 47 runs through the
beautiful Sirhowy Valley Country
Park. This stretch follows an
old dismantled railway line.

The Bristol Channel at St Brides, Wentlooge
The broad and featureless coastline here gives an uninterrupted view of the North Somerset coast.

Coast at St Brides, Wentlooge
The levels here are heavily dyked for drainage and the shore runs flat and straight from Cardiff to
Newport along the banks of the River Severn and Bristol Channel.

Skirrid Mountain
In Welsh, Ysgyryd Fawr, the Skirrid is
a well known landmark near Abergavenny.

Tintern Abbey and Old Railway Bridge

Tintern Abbey Close Up

Tintern Abbey
If ever an abbey was situated
in a more picturesque setting
I have yet to discover it.

Tintern Abbey in the Fog

Mist in the Wye Valley near Tintern

Tintern Abbey Mill
This is the site of the old mill, now gift shops and a restaurant attract visitors.

Tintern Parva Railway Station
The old Wye Valley railway station has been 'converted' to a delightful picnic site and tearoom,
with, nearby, a collection of fascinating wooden sculptures of characters from local history.

Tintern Parva Carvings
The wooden carvings of local heroes
(factual and mythical) are to be found at the
Tintern Parva Railway Station

Eleanor of Provence

Geoffrey of Monmouth

King Offa

St Tewdrig

Tintern Village

This pretty 'Wyeside' village clings to the western side of the River Wye between the water and high wooded cliffs. It is, unfortunately, prone to some pretty serious flooding from time to time.

Wye Swans near Tintern

Raglan Castle
This magnificent late medieval ruin is popular with visitors and has been used as a film set for several productions, including 'Time Bandit'. What an ignominious end for a castle with such a history attached to it!

Raglan Castle
The castle was so well built that attempts to demolish the Great Tower singularly failed,
only two walls being affected – mind you, the demolition crew were using pickaxes!

Tintern Parva – Railway Carriages
These old carriages provide an information centre relating to the railway line, now long gone, and a gift shop.

Signal Box
The old signal box now houses an art gallery with exhibitions held regularly of local art and photography.

Sugarloaf from Llangattock Escarpment
This was photographed on a superb autumn day
when the air was really crisp and clear.

Three Stones, Trellech
Just outside the village, the Three Stones stand in a row
with, no doubt, many tales to tell if only they could.

Trellech Village

Photographed on a cold and frosty morning, the view over Trellech extends right across to the
Wye Valley with morning mist rising in the distance.

Shop in Usk
I was struck by the lovely way that this shop spilled out onto the pavement to attract passers by.

Clock Tower, Usk
This elegant brick tower with its clean white clock, somehow just complements the little rural town of Usk.

Wye Valley

Photographed from near the 365 Steps, this evening view looks across the valley farmland just above Chepstow. On the right the first Severn Bridge is just visible.

Wintour's Leap

Strictly speaking this is in Gloucestershire but was photographed from Monmouthshire! The story goes that Sir John Wintour,
a Royalist, was being pursued to the point where he leapt over the cliff and landed safely in the River Wye below.
Were he to try that today his fate would be clearer cut – the river has since altered its course.

Second Severn Crossing
I was working in Bristol when this bridge was under construction and watched its progress daily.
What a superb piece of civil engineering!

GR 7/09